I0236459

CATHOLIC NURSERY RHYMES

Jesus at prayer with His Blessed Mother and St. Joseph

CATHOLIC NURSERY RHYMES

A Life of Our Blessed Lord in Verse
for Young Children

by Sister Mary Gertrude, M.A.

Sisters of Charity, Convent, New Jersey

2018

ST. AUGUSTINE ACADEMY PRESS
HOMER GLEN, ILLINOIS

Nihil Obstat
ARTHUR J. SCANLAN, S.T.D.
Censor Librorum

Imprimatur
✠ PATRICK, CARDINAL HAYES
Archbishop of New York

NEW YORK, July 15, 1925

To
CHARLES RICHARD QUINLAN
one of Christ's little friends
these rhymes are affectionately dedicated

ISBN: 978-1-64051-070-8

A is for Angel,
  St. Gabriel fair,
Who appeared as Our Lady
  was kneeling in prayer,
And told her that Mother
  of God she would be.
"Hail Mary!" he whispered;
  "The Lord is with thee."

B is for Bethlehem,
  dear little town!
As the birthplace of Jesus
  it has great renown.
For there, when His Mother
  was duly enrolled,
Our sweet little Saviour
  was born in the cold.

C is the Cave.

See the ox and the sheep,
And the straw where the Infant
is lying asleep.
Mary and Joseph
are kneeling in prayer,
And poor men, called shepherds,
also are there.

D is the Death
   which King Herod now planned
For all the boy-babies
   who lived in his land.
He hated the newly-born
   King of the Jews,
Fearing in time
   his own kingdom to lose.

E is for East.
Three wise men there were,
Who brought from their countries
gold, incense and myrrh.
At the side of the manger,
they knelt down to pray;
Then returned to their homes
by a different way.

F is for Flight
  to a far-distant land.
"To Egypt depart"
  was the angel's command.
Though painful the journey,
  at once they obeyed,
And seven long years
  in that country they stayed.

G is for God,
  Who made you and me,
The sun, moon and stars,
  the earth and the sea.
He is everywhere present,
  Three Persons in One;
The Second came down
  and became Mary's Son.

H is for Home.

It is Nazareth at last,
Where with His parents
　His boyhood was passed.
"He was subject to them,"
　for He always obeyed,
And practised with Joseph
　the Carpenter's trade.

I for Instruction.

When only a boy
He taught the wise doctors,
  who listened with joy.
In the Temple He lingered
  the law to explain,
While for three days His Mother
  was searching in vain.

J for His Name,
   so revered and so blest;
Of all names we utter,
   'tis holiest, best.
Whenever you hear it,
   wherever it's said,
You must show your devotion
   by bowing your head.

K is for Kindness.
When grown to a man,
He left His dear home,
    and His life-work began.
The little ones loved Him
    so gentle was He,
Saying, "Suffer the children
    to come unto Me."

L is for Learners,
poor men, twelve in all,
Apostles who left
all they had at His call.
They learned His great doctrine,
then taught in His name.
Their chief was St. Peter.
First Pope he became.

M is for Miracles.

See the great crowd
Which everywhere followed Him,
   crying aloud.
He cured their diseases,
   gave life to their dead,
While the fame of His power
   through all the land spread.

N is for New Law,
   replacing the Old,
Which at the Last Supper
   so sweetly He told,---
The New Law of love
   which induced Him to leave
His body and blood
   which we daily receive.

O is for Olivet,
  lonely and drear.
The supper is over,
  His Passion draws near.
He sweats blood to suffer
  for your sins and mine,
And prays to His Father,
  "Not My will, but Thine."

P is for Pilate,
   the judge on his throne.
Christ stands before him,
   accused by His own.
"Condemn Him to death!"
   the rude mob demands;
Then Pilate delivers Him
   into their hands.

Q for Quadrangle,
  a courtyard enclosed;
To suffering and insult
  Our Lord was exposed.
They scourged Him, and pressed
  on His head a sharp crown
Then hailed Him as King,
  and to mock Him, knelt down.

R for Redeemer,
  so patient and sweet,
As He carries His cross
    through the rough, crowded
      street.
Beneath it He falls;
  with His blood it is stained,
Yet He shoulders it bravely
  till Calvary is gained.

S is for Sacrifice.
  nailed between thieves,
Three hours He hangs,
  while His dear Mother grieves.
At length "it is finished";
  His life-work is done;
Christ dies on the cross,
  and redemption is won.

T is for Tomb.

In a rock it was made.
Within it Our Lord's
   sacred body was laid.
See! Mary is leaving
   the place where He died,
Departing in sorrow,
   St. John at her side.

U is for souls
　　Unredeemed, and denied
An entrance to heaven
　　till Jesus had died.
In Limbo they waited
　　in longing and prayer.
Our Lord's soul descended
　　to comfort them there.

V is for Victor.

At dawn the third day,
The tomb became bright,
  and the stone rolled away.
Disfigured no longer,
  but beautiful, bright,
Christ rose from the dead,
  and appeared in His might.

W the Welcome,
   that waited above
For Him Who redeemed us
   with infinite love.
"I go to make ready
   a place for My friends,"---
And while He is speaking,
   behold! He ascends.

X is for Ten;
  it is used as a sign.
The Ten great Commandments
  our duties define.
The Church is our Mother,
  and teaches us, too;
Her laws are but six,
  and are binding, though few.

Y is for You, for whom
all this was done.
Your body will die,
  but your soul will live on.
Do all the Church teaches,
  and love our dear Lord;
Then heaven will be
  your eternal reward.

Z With this letter
the alphabet ends.
Our story is finished
for Christ's little friends.
Some day through the earth
will be heard a loud blast,---
THE END OF THE WORLD!
day of judgment at last!